Who Lives on...
THE PRAIRIE?

Who Lives on... THE PRAIRIE?

Ron Hirschi

Photographs by
Galen Burrell

A *WHERE ANIMALS LIVE* BOOK

G.P. Putnam's Sons   New York

Library of Congress Cataloging-in-Publication Data
Hirschi, Ron. Who lives on—the prairie?/Ron Hirschi;
photographs by Galen Burrell. p. cm.—(A Where animals
live book) Summary: Text and photographs introduce
the sights and sounds of life on the prairie, including the
prairie dog, dancing birds, and long-tailed weasel.
1. Prairie fauna—Juvenile literature.   2. Prairie
fauna—United States—Juvenile literature.   [1. Prairie
animals.]   I. Burrell, Galen, ill.   II. Title.   III. Series.
QL115.H57 1989   591.52′643—dc19   87-25159   CIP   AC
ISBN 0-399-21901-3
First impression

In memory of Poppa—
who saw the bison shadows

Watch
for the
prairie dog family,
listen for the
dancing birds,

and follow
the long-tailed
weasel's trail as
it disappears in
the flowers
and thick
prairie
grass.

The weasel hunts
for mice.

So does a hungry coyote
that pounces at each
rustle in the
grass.

Suddenly, the coyote stops.
What does it see?

Is it mother skunk,
sniffing the trail
for breakfast?

Is it baby rabbit,
hiding in the
grass?

Is it the meadowlark's golden feathers?

No,
it is a
burrowing owl,
silently watching
the coyote from
its morning
perch.

When the coyote vanishes over the hill, the owl flies to a burrow that looks just right for a nest.

Does someone already live here?

Yes,
it is the
prairie dog family.
They scurry from their den
when the owl flies off
to search for a home
all its own.

Mother prairie dog
gathers straw for
her nest...

while others
munch bluegrass
and prickly pear cactus,

then greet one another with
a prairie dog embrace
and a prairie dog
kiss.

Yip!
A prairie dog
barks a loud alarm
as, *whoosh!*, a golden
eagle swoops down
from the sky and sends
the prairie dogs diving
into the safety of
their burrow.

As the eagle soars away,
it circles the tall cottonwood trees
along a prairie creek.

Here, hidden from the eagle's view
a white-tailed deer fawn hides
in the shade, waiting for
its mother to return.

Out in the open prairie,
a pronghorn fawn hides from
danger by staying so still you
could not see it breathing.

Whooo! Whooo! Whooo!
What is that ghostly sound rising
from beyond the pronghorn's
hiding place?

It is the dancing birds
—prairie chickens, leaping and strutting.

Watch the males stomp their feet,
flash their bright red air sacs,
and flare their feather horns
as a female watches
in silence.

Then, close your eyes
and imagine a time when
this prairie was vast and the
land thundered beneath the feet
of so many bison that you
could never count
them all.

AFTERWORD
for Parents and Teachers,
Big Brothers and Sisters

Today, it is far more common to see a beautifully feathered shrike sitting on a wire stretched across a plowed field than to see the wonderful dance of the prairie chicken. The shrike and many other animals have adapted to some of the changes that have destroyed much of one of the earth's greatest treasures—our native prairie with its millions of bison, pronghorn, and prairie chickens.

It is almost impossible to believe that little more than a hundred years ago, numbers of bison alone outnumbered the enormous herds of African wildebeest by at least ten times. In one corner of Texas, known as the Staked Plains, an estimated 400 million prairie dogs once lived in a vast prairie dog "city." Now they are disappearing due to many causes. Prairie chickens also numbered in the millions and have declined at increasing rates in recent years.

You can still see bison in Yellowstone National Park. Watch for prairie dogs in Alberta, Montana, Wyoming, and Colorado. And, search for the lesser prairie chicken in the springtime when they perform their elaborate courtship dance in places such as the Comanche National Grasslands in Colorado, the Northeast corner of New Mexico, and in scattered parts of West Texas, Kansas, and Oklahoma.

We hope this introduction to prairie wildlife will encourage you to learn more about the prairie and the urgent needs of many vanishing prairie animals.